MW01134437

Fibromyalgia

God's Grace for Chronic
Pain Sufferers

Robert Smith

New
Growth
Press

www.newgrowthpress.com

223- 5438

New Growth Press, Greensboro, NC 27404
www.newgrowthpress.com
Copyright © 2012 by Robert Smith.

All Scripture quotations, unless otherwise indicated, are taken from the *New American Standard Bible*, © Copyright 1960, 1962, 1963, 1968, 1971, 1972, 1973, 1975, 1977, 1995 by The Lockman Foundation. Used by permission.

Scripture quotations marked ESV are taken from the *Holy Bible, English Standard Version*® (ESV®), copyright © 2000, 2001 by Crossway Bibles, a division of Good News Publishers. Used by permission. All rights reserved.

Cover Design: Tandem Creative, Tom Temple, tandemcreative.net
Typesetting: Lisa Parnell, lparnell.com

ISBN-13: 978-1-938267-93-2
ISBN-13: 978-1-938267-40-6 (eBook)

Library of Congress Cataloging-in-Publication Data
Smith, Robert, 1929–
  Fibromyalgia : God's grace for chronic pain sufferers / Robert Smith.
     p. cm.
  Includes bibliographical references and index.
  ISBN-13: 978-1-938267-93-2 (alk. paper)
  1. Chronic pain—Patients—Religious life. 2. Chronic pain—Religious aspects—Christianity. 3. Fibromyalgia—Patients—Religious life. 4. Fibromyalgia—Religious aspects—Christianity. I. Title.
  BV4910.337.S65   2012
  248.8'6196742—dc23
                                                    2012027947

Printed in Canada

19 18 17 16 15 14 13 12   1 2 3 4 5

" I have suffered with horrible pain for years," explained Susan. "My physician diagnosed me with a condition called fibromyalgia." Susan's diagnosis refers to her chronic physical pain, but she also experiences great emotional pain from having to miss her son's soccer games or her daughter's concerts because her body is in agony. Her absence from important events and her seeming inconsistency has often brought criticism from her coworkers, friends, and family. Susan frequently feels frustrated by the skeptical and insensitive responses she receives when she explains her condition. This lack of compassion toward her is intensified by her own feelings of disappointment with her life. She feels hindered from being the person she wants to be and from doing the activities she enjoys most. Her desire to be an attentive wife, an involved mother, an accomplished employee, and a skilled servant seem foolish and hopeless. Susan wants answers but can't seem to find them.

Do you identify with Susan's story? If so, take comfort that answers can be found. Even though you won't find fibromyalgia mentioned in the Bible, God has much to say to those who are suffering. He wants you to come to him with all of your questions, doubts, and fears and then trust his love and grace for you. You will find that his promises in the Bible give you hope and direction in the midst of your suffering. To better understand what those promises are and how they apply to your condition, let's start with what is known (and not known) about fibromyalgia.

Understanding Fibromyalgia

Medical professionals estimate that less than 5 percent of the U.S. population has fibromyalgia, and that it affects approximately four times more women than men[1] between the ages of twenty and fifty.[2] The name *fibromyalgia* is a medical term made up of three parts. *Fibro-* refers to connective tissue; *my-* means muscle; *-algia* means pain. Thus, the word literally means "connective tissue muscle pain."

This is appropriate since the primary symptom of fibromyalgia is chronic pain. Patients experience pain in varying degrees of severity that can get better or worse from one day to the next. They also report having chronic pain for most, if not all, of their lives.[3] Interestingly, no permanent damage to the body seems to accompany this ongoing pain.

The major criterion for a diagnosis of fibromyalgia is the complaint of generalized pain or pain in many areas of the body. So if your doctor has given you this diagnosis, it is likely that he based his evaluation on when your pain started, what has aggravated and lessened your pain, your previous methods of treatment, and your history of other medical conditions. The doctor may have done a physical examination to find any obvious physical problems that may have caused your symptoms and that could be treated. In the case of fibromyalgia, it is unlikely that other problems were found (as will be explained in a moment). Laboratory tests are usually done for the purpose of uncovering and ruling out diseases that require specific treatment.

Initially, your diagnosis may have alleviated your fears that cancer or some other life-threatening disease was present, but then you found yourself with the unanswered question of what causes this painful condition. Much research has been done looking for answers. Many proposed causes have been presented in scientific and nonscientific literature, and many theories have been developed to explain the symptoms. However, to date, no consistent or specific cause has been found, and no theory has been proven to be factual. If you read or hear of some alleged cause of fibromyalgia, don't be fooled. No consistent evidence for disease (a proven abnormality causing the symptoms) has been produced from the extensive research performed. If a proven cause is found, it will be widely reported.

The absence of a proven cause does not mean the pain is "all in your head." On the contrary, researchers have concluded that the pain you are experiencing is real, which of course you already know! However, just because the pain is real does not necessarily mean your body has a disease. People often erroneously conclude that any symptom of pain means a disease is present. This may or may not be the case. With fibromyalgia, pain signals originate in the connective tissue and pass through nerves to the spinal cord and from there to the brain where they are interpreted. However, researchers have not found any connective tissue disorder to explain the pain. The current leading theory is that fibromyalgia patients have abnormalities in the way the brain processes pain signals, which has motivated researchers to study the effects of thinking on pain. In truth, modern science cannot explain every symptom the human body experiences—not yet.

Because there is no proven cause for fibromyalgia, you will hear of many different recommended treatments. However, none of these treatments have proven to be consistently beneficial for all people with fibromyalgia. While the FDA has approved several drugs for use in treating fibromyalgia, most physicians are aware that medications alone are not the answer. Some researchers think small doses of antidepressants may reduce pain, so your doctor may recommend these. But although your fibromyalgia symptoms are real, there is no known cure.

As Christians, we do know that any malfunction in our bodies is due to the fall in some way. Sin resulted from the failure of the first humans to obey their Creator. Adam and Eve decided to go their own way and do what they thought was best, instead of trust and obey God. Their disobedience brought brokenness and death to all that God had created. This brokenness affects both the spiritual and the physical; therefore our bodies will never function without some problems. Many unpleasant symptoms cannot be easily linked to a physical abnormality, but we can be sure that sin is at the root. This is the case with fibromyalgia. *This does not mean that your individual sin is the cause of your pain.* It means that the overall brokenness of creation will include physical brokenness until Christ returns.

At this point, it would be easy to conclude that your situation is hopeless, both from a physical and a spiritual perspective. But it isn't! Believers throughout the ages have suffered from physical problems that medicine could not solve. God was present with each of them in their suffering and offered them one of his greatest gifts—faith. Despite pain and difficult circumstances, they lived with hope. As you go to him, God will also help you and give you hope. Perhaps not in the ways you might want or expect, but he will answer you as you go to him. God's grace will fill your life as your relationship with him deepens. Your suffering cannot separate you from God's love and mercy. Instead, as you go to him with your struggles, you will know him and his love more deeply.

God's Grace Gives Meaning to Your Suffering

When we are in pain and relief seems far away, it's easy to think that we are just pawns in God's cosmic plan. This makes suffering feel even worse because it seems pointless. Perhaps you are wondering:

- Why is life so unfair?
- How could this possibly be in God's plan?
- Why do other people seem to have easier lives?

These are questions people often ask when life is hard and they are trying to make sense of it. But don't forget that God is always doing something in the intimate details of our lives. He knows us perfectly, which includes knowing how we suffer and how it affects us. Although everyone in this world suffers in some way, those who trust God find that knowing him in the midst of suffering brings the grace to endure and the faith to see beyond their suffering to God's purposes. God's grace is not absent in your life or stopped by your suffering. The opposite is true—in your suffering you will see even more of God's grace. Below are some specific ways that God's grace is revealed in suffering. As you read, ask God to show himself and his ways to you. Perhaps right now you are in too much pain to read this whole minibook. If so, just take it one paragraph at a time and ask God to show you his grace and mercy as you consider these truths.

The Grace of Knowing Jesus in Your Suffering

When you are suffering, it's hard to focus on anything. But here's a simple truth for you to remember every day that will bring God's grace into your life: Jesus is a man of sorrows, acquainted with suffering (Isaiah 53:3). When you turn to Jesus in your suffering, you are going to someone who understands and knows what it is like to suffer. He promises to be with you through your suffering and he says that *nothing* can separate you from God's love (Romans 8:35–38).

Because the One who is a man of sorrows is with you, your suffering will not separate you from him but draw you closer.

Take a moment to think about what Jesus suffered. His suffering was not confined to the time he spent on the cross. The suffering of Jesus began the minute he was made flesh. Jesus' entire human existence was a form of suffering because his godhood was limited to a human body. "Although he was a son, he learned obedience through what he suffered" (Hebrews 5:8 ESV). He is not indifferent to our suffering, because he has experienced it to a degree we can't even imagine. Since Jesus has come and suffered on our behalf, we have an intimacy with him that before was only hoped for. His Spirit dwells within us, and we know he understands what we are experiencing.

The Grace of Becoming Like Jesus in Your Suffering

Becoming closer to Jesus means you will become more like him. That is another important way you will see God's grace at work in your suffering. Your suffering isn't wasted. God uses every circumstance in your life, including your fibromyalgia, to grow you like Jesus. That is part of the "good" that Paul is talking about below when he says "all things" work together for good to those who love God.

> And we know that God causes all things to
> work together for good to those who love

God, to those who are called according to
His purpose. For those whom He foreknew,
He also predestined to become conformed to
the image of His Son, that He might be the
firstborn among many brethren. (Romans
8:28–29)

The "all" of this passage includes every physical
problem we can and will experience. This means what-
ever God might allow, even physical problems, is for
the purpose of helping us to become more like Christ
and to know his love for us.

Experiencing pain is part of becoming more like
Christ. Christ suffered out of love for those who were
his enemies. Instead of making us pay for our wrongs,
he took our penalty so we could live. His act of sacrifice
not only saves us, it proves his goodness and willing-
ness to love even at the cost of his life. When you turn
away from hopelessness and turn to God, you do "share
his sufferings" (Philippians 3:10 ESV). The more you
see your own suffering as just a small taste of what Jesus
went through for you, the more you will taste the comfort of his love. When you face your suffering with this
understanding, your life can shine with God's glory as
you become more like Jesus. We always become like
our closest friends. As you grow closer to Jesus, your
life will shine with his love.

Becoming more like Christ means that you will
have more of the fruit of the Spirit (Galatians 5:22–23),

which is a great gift. For example, God may use your fibromyalgia, an illness that does not respond quickly to treatment, to help you grow in patience toward God and the people trying to help you. When you deal with your weakness and lack of medical answers by asking for help from your Father in heaven, you put on more of the character and mind of Christ, who depended on the Father for everything.

Although it might be easy to think that your pain means God has forgotten you, the opposite is actually true. He has called you to walk with him down a path of suffering so that you will know him and love him. Can you think of other ways that God is making you more like Jesus as you struggle with pain and weakness? Ask God to show you what he is doing in your life in the midst of suffering and pain. Ask others to pray that, instead of hopelessness, you would see the ways God is drawing you closer to Jesus and making you like him in the midst of your suffering.

The Grace to Shine Like Jesus in Suffering

Pain is very distressing. It's natural to try to avoid pain and easy to take the next step of making pain relief the primary focus of your life. But God wants to free you to focus on something even more valuable—knowing and shining with his glory. This doesn't diminish your pain and struggle with fibromyalgia. Instead, it gives meaning to your struggle. Jesus makes this point in John 16:21 when he describes the pain of childbirth.

"Whenever a woman is in labor she has pain, because her hour has come; but when she gives birth to the child, she no longer remembers the anguish because of the joy that a child has been born into the world." Jesus helps us understand that the difficulties of life are not meaningless. Labor is extremely painful, but when the baby is born, the focus is on the baby, not the pain. The gain is superior to the pain.

What might the "gain" be in your suffering? In God's perfect economy, pain can produce benefits. Not because pain is good, but because God is good. Even with a condition like fibromyalgia that has only symptoms and no known physical cause, God's glory shines with hope and meaning. In fact, the more meaningless something may appear, the greater the glory produced when God reveals himself. Imagine the glory when Jesus returns and answers every "why Lord?" that has been uttered.

But God's glory will not only be revealed in answers to our questions. God's glory is something we get to *be*. Paul makes it clear what an amazing treasure this glory is when he says, "For I consider that the sufferings of this present time are not worthy to be compared with the glory that is to be revealed to us" (Romans 8:18). He makes the contrast even more vivid in 2 Corinthians 4:17: "For momentary, light affliction is producing for us an eternal weight of glory far beyond all comparison." Your present sufferings produce an incomparable glory in your future that is eternal and heavy and beyond anything you can imagine. It is so wonderful that even though your present suffering is extremely difficult and unremitting, Paul tells you it is temporary and light.

Of course, even as you trust in God that these things are true, you will still desire relief from pain. In the garden of Gethsemane Christ asks for relief from pain, even as he trusts and obeys his Father's will for him. Jesus knows his Father doesn't delight in his suffering. This motivates him to ask for relief while simultaneously trusting him when suffering is what he's asked to endure.

Shining with God's glory can begin now as you ask God for help in responding by faith to your struggle. In Matthew 5:16, Christ calls you to "let your light shine before men in such a way that they may see your good works, and glorify your Father who is in heaven." God gives each of us different ways to shine for his glory. What this looks like for you will be different from those who are in good health. Your faithful responses to your pain will demonstrate to others your Father's goodness and grace. When the pain and fatigue become great, you can depend on God's grace. This brings glory to God and pleases him, and it will show those around you the difference faith makes in the midst of suffering.

God's glory is seen in the difference between our natural response to pain and difficult circumstances and the response of faith. It's an amazing thing for those around you to see faith on display even in the midst of pain and weakness. As you ask God for grace, his Spirit will be at work to help you. Even the smallest things—patiently waiting for a doctor to return your call, displaying a quiet spirit as you wait for help, praying for someone else despite your weakness, responding without frustration when others misunderstand your struggle with fibromyalgia—are not small in God's world. Each time you respond to the pain and frustration of fibromyalgia with faith and love, you shine with the glory of God. Only God could change your natural reactions of hopelessness and frustration to faith and love.

Remember "God is able to make all grace abound to you, so that having all sufficiency in all things at all times, you may abound in every good work" (2 Corinthians 9:8 esv). The blessings you receive by glorifying God will far outweigh the physical pain you experience.

Please do not understand this as minimizing your suffering. One of God's purposes in suffering is to help us grow in dependence on him. The reality is that we need him for every breath we take. When we suffer, we lean on him more; we experience the joy of knowing him more deeply; and we shine with his glory even in the midst of our daily struggles.

As you think about your struggle with fibromyalgia, remember God gives benefits that can't be measured by the senses. Responding to your pain with faith and love brings glory to God and is the utmost benefit to you. God "has designed his eternal purpose so that his glory and our good are inextricably bound together."[4]

Job's story of faithfulness to God in the midst of extreme suffering is still comforting and encouraging God's people today. Job's suffering and grief were not wasted because his story has given people through the centuries a picture of faith in God that was not crushed by disappointing circumstances. Also, remember Jesus' ministry from the cross in his agonizing pain. Faithfulness to God—even when it hurts—speaks volumes.

Take a moment to think about whom in your life you can share God's love and faithfulness with. You might feel there is little you can do as you suffer, but when you ask God to show you who to minister to, he will help you. In your distress, you can remember to pray for others in distress. Perhaps you can write a short note, email, or text to encourage a friend. Even accepting help with thankfulness is a significant way to minister to others.

Look to Jesus for Daily Grace

The apostle Paul was no stranger to suffering. As he traveled the ancient world preaching the gospel he was beaten, stoned, shipwrecked, and imprisoned. In the following passage what he shares about suffering comes from personal experience.

Who will separate us from the love of Christ? Will tribulation, or distress, or persecution, or famine, or nakedness, or peril, or sword? Just as it is written, "For your sake we are being put to death all day long; We were considered as sheep to be slaughtered." But in all these things we overwhelmingly conquer through Him who loved us. (Romans 8:35–37)

Paul lists many categories of suffering. The suffering is so great that it may even seem that life is not worth living. Like sheep dragged to the slaughterhouse, it seems there is no escape. But Paul reveals an exciting truth that *in* all these situations you can overwhelmingly conquer. So the question becomes how to "overwhelmingly conquer" in the middle of an unremitting, unrelieved pain that has an unknown cause. The answer is "through him who loved us."

Severe pain can make it difficult to think about anything other than obtaining relief. Yet God's grace enables you to depend on Jesus and live for him even when pain demands your attention. That grace comes to us in daily increments as we ask. In Exodus, the Israelites were in the wilderness without means of obtaining food (Exodus 16). God provided special food called manna that appeared in the morning like dew and was only edible for one day. Just as he did for the Israelites, God will provide all you need one day at a time, maybe even one minute or second at a time. Rather than look at a long bleak future with unrelenting pain, look to Jesus for grace for the moment ahead.

Jesus is the one who loves you and who will help you "overwhelmingly conquer" as you depend on him for daily grace. Be assured that God doesn't have just a small supply of daily grace for you. God has promised you so much grace that Paul describes it as abounding or overflowing (2 Corinthians 9:8).

More than one patient has told me, "I don't take pain well." The reality is that we all have a natural fear of pain and rarely take it well. But God's grace can free us from this fear by helping us focus on his goodness in the middle of pain. God's grace comes to each of us as we go to him with faith and ask him for the daily help we need with the daily trouble we experience. He will answer us when we call out to him.

This does not mean you should avoid seeking medical help for symptom relief. However, keep the pursuit of relief in its proper place. Relief is a powerful motivator, but God intends for you to seek him first (Matthew 6:33). It would be easy to allow your desire for relief to dominate your thoughts, actions, money management. But seek the Lord first and ask him for the grace to live for him in the midst of your pain, which will help you keep the pursuit of relief in perspective and in line with being faithful with what God's given you. Below are some ways to help you look to Jesus for daily grace.

Depending on God's Promises

As we noted earlier, those who struggle with fibromyalgia suffer from generalized pain. Because the discomfort is so great, it can become easy to fear the pain and worry about how bad it will be on any particular day. It's important for you, throughout each day, to actively trust in God's promises. Paul calls this taking "every thought captive to obey Christ" (2 Corinthians 10:5 ESV).

Learning to take every thought captive might sound strange to you. But it just means learning to replace your worried and hopeless thoughts with God's true and reliable promises. When your thoughts are full of fear and discouragement about what you are experiencing now or might experience in the future, ask God to help you replace those thoughts with these promises:

- God promises to be with me in my suffering. He promises never to leave me (Hebrews 13:5).
- Jesus wants me to go to him in my suffering. He is my great High Priest who has conquered death and now continually intercedes for his people (Hebrews 7:24–25).
- Jesus rules over all things so I have nothing to fear. He willingly experienced pain for me when he took my penalty on the cross so that I could be made righteous (1 Peter 3:18; 2 Corinthians 5:21).
- God is in control of all things and his control is good (Proverbs 21:1; Psalms 119:68; 136:1).
- God has promised that because I love him, everything (including any pain I experience) is

for my good to make me more like his precious Son (Romans 8:28–29).

- God promises that he will never give me more than I can handle spiritually without also providing ways to handle my suffering with growing obedience (1 Corinthians 10:13).

Take a moment and list all of your fears, worries, and struggles. Then look again at God's promises to you and write a specific promise and Bible verse next to each of your struggles. Don't try to do this all at once. Even if once a week you write out one of God's promises and apply it to what you are experiencing, you will see God's grace flow into your life as you fill your mind with God's promises of care and love for you. You can do this every time your anxious thoughts threaten to overwhelm you.

Ask the Spirit to bring these promises to your mind so that you can focus on God's grace and help rather than your discomfort. I know this sounds difficult, but as you ask him to make his care, his presence, and his help the focus of your thinking and conversation, he will do that. This is a prayer that the Father always answers with a yes.

Focusing on God's promises rather than your pain will certainly have spiritual benefits for you, but it may have physical benefits as well. All of us experience difficulties that bring stress into our lives. Some pressures may be minor irritations of everyday life, such as alarm clock failure, traffic congestion, long checkout lines, and unhappy children. Other pressures are major issues, such as chronic pain. How we respond to any of these difficulties has a physical affect on our bodies. For example, becoming upset and stressed because of daily pressures can produce painful cramps in the muscles of the intestinal tract. The pain may be as severe as the pain caused by an inflammation of the intestine. In either case, the muscles cramp and produce pain. Intestinal cramps (not caused by inflammation) and fibromyalgia are not at all the same, but the similarity is that disease cannot be found in either case. Changing the response to stress has helped to reduce these cramps and may also lessen the pain associated with fibromyalgia. You may find that "taking every thought captive" by turning to Christ in your fear and discouragement will change your response to the stress of fibromyalgia and strengthen you physically as well as spiritually.

Depending on God's Power in Your Weakness

Like you, the apostle Paul also suffered from a debilitating condition that left him weak and needy. He called his suffering a "thorn in the flesh." Paul cried out to God for relief, as I'm sure you have many times. Here is how he talked to God and how God responded to him:

> Three times I pleaded with the Lord about
> this, that it should leave me. But he said

to me, "My grace is sufficient for you, for my power is made perfect in weakness." Therefore I will boast all the more gladly of my weaknesses, so that the power of Christ may rest upon me. For the sake of Christ, then, I am content with weaknesses, insults, hardships, persecutions, and calamities. For when I am weak, then I am strong. (2 Corinthians 12:8–10 ESV)

Paul specifically prayed for his malady to be removed, but God's answer was to provide him with grace in his weakness. God explained to Paul that human weakness unleashed God's power. Paul understood that Christ loved him and allowed his "thorn" to continue for his spiritual benefit, so that Paul would know even more of God's power in his life. He understood that the benefits of suffering were connected to Christ's love for him and his love for Christ. When you are faithful to God in spite of weakness, this demonstrates the power of God rather than your own power.

Because Paul understood this, he was content to depend on God's grace and be strengthened in weakness. He truly was powerful because he relied on God's power instead of his own strength, which he knew would always fail at some point. God's power never fails and is made perfect in your weakness. The Lord of life and the Creator of the universe is promising that his power is sufficient for you. Relying on God's power instead of your own brings a deep security into your life that you could never provide for yourself.

Remembering Your True Home

After Adam and Eve fell, our world radically changed. Sin not only impacted human life, but also the world in which we live. Today our beautiful world is broken and twisted. We all have to face the reality that we live in a broken world with sickness, disease, wars, strife, and struggle. That is one of the reasons the Bible speaks of heaven so often. It is comforting to know that the home we live in today is not as good as it gets. In fact, our lives on earth are actually quite short. The Bible often describes the shortness of life in vivid terms. Psalm 39:5 describes it as a breath; James 4:14 as a vapor or mist that quickly vanishes; 1 Peter 1:24 as a grass or flower that withers; Psalm 102:11 as a shadow that is here and then gone.

In addition to the shortness of life on earth, the Bible speaks of the glories of heaven—our true and lasting home. Revelation 21:4 mentions glories that seem to speak directly to those with fibromyalgia: "And he shall wipe away every tear from their eyes; and there will no longer be any death; there will no longer be any mourning, or crying, or *pain*; the first things have passed away" (emphasis added).

We all need to remember that God has prepared a place for us (John 14), and that place is free from all the challenges and difficulties of this life. You may have to suffer for a while, but you have a God who reminds you that the temporary challenges of today will be replaced with the eternal glories of tomorrow. In your pain, you can earnestly cry, "Come, Lord Jesus!" (Revelation 22:20).

God in his grace provides healing for some people and may actually remove the symptoms altogether. This may be through the natural healing process he has created in human bodies or through medications. For some, there may be symptom relief. For others, there may be no significant relief. We should ask for this kind of healing and appeal to God's mercy to grant it because we know he can do it. But along with that prayer, we should also pray for a heart that will submit to what God has for us.

In this life everyone will contend with varying types of body breakdown. In heaven we will have perfect bodies that will last forever. Your new resurrected body will be free from all the ailments and pains of this life. In addition, you will be in the presence of your Savior and all the glories of heaven. What a wonderful destination awaits!

God does not promise pain-free lives, and everyone suffers in some way. But if you remember that you have a God who knows and loves you, and who uses his power to free you and bring you nearer to him, you will handle suffering in ways you never thought possible. As you learn to invite God into your suffering more and more, you will experience a renewed freedom that pain will not impede. May God bless you as you trust him through the challenge of fibromyalgia, and may he give you the grace to say along with Paul, "For I consider that the sufferings of this present time are not worthy to be compared with the glory that is to be revealed to us" (Romans 8:18).

Endnotes

1. Srinivas G. Rao, MD, PhD; Judith F. Gendreau, MD; Jay D. Kranzler, MD, PhD; "Understanding the Fibromyalgia Syndrome," *Medscape Today*, 06 March 2008. http://www.medscape.com/viewarticle/569749?src=nl_crb.

2. John Buckner Winfield, MD, "Fibromyalgia," *Medscape Reference*, Updated 20 December 2011. http://emedicine.medscape.com/article/329838-overview.

3. S. B. Milan, "Fibromyalgia: When the patient hurts all over," *Family Practice Recertification*, vol. 18, 1996, 92.

4. Jerry Bridges, *Trusting God* (Colorado Springs: NavPress, 1989), 26.